The Dream World

BOOKS BY ALISON PICK

POETRY
Question & Answer (2003)
The Dream World (2008)

FICTION
The Sweet Edge (2005)

The Dream World

ALISON PICK

McCLELLAND & STEWART

COPYRIGHT © 2008 BY ALISON PICK

All rights reserved. The use of any part of this publication reproduced, transmitted in any form or by any means, electronic, mechanical, photocopying, recording, orotherwise, or stored in a retrieval system, without the prior written consent of the publisher – or, in case of photocopying or other reprographic copying, a licence from the Canadian Copyright Licensing Agency – is an infringement of the copyright law.

LIBRARY AND ARCHIVES CANADA CATALOGUING IN PUBLICATION

Pick, Alison
The dream world : poems / Alison Pick.

ISBN 978-0-7710-7046-4

I. Title.

PS8581.I2563D74 2008   C811'.6   C2007-906591-0

We acknowledge the financial support of the Government of Canada through the Book Publishing Industry Development Program and that of the Government of Ontario through the Ontario Media Development Corporation's Ontario Book Initiative. We further acknowledge the support of the Canada Council for the Arts and the Ontario Arts Council for our publishing program.

Typeset in Mrs Eaves by M&S, Toronto
Printed and bound in Canada

This book is printed on acid-free paper that is
100% recycled, ancient-forest friendly.

McClelland & Stewart Ltd.
75 Sherbourne Street
Toronto, Ontario
M5A 2P9
www.mcclelland.com

2 3 4 5   12 11 10 09 08

When at last they awoke, it was already dark night. Gretel began to cry and said: "How are we to get out of the forest now?" But Hansel comforted her and said: "Just wait a little, until the moon has risen, and then we will find the way."

— THE BROTHERS GRIMM

The dream is the small hidden door...

— C.G. JUNG

CONTENTS

ALONE IN THE WOODS FOR THE REST OF THE WINTER
    The Hinterland *3*
    Full Moon: Reading "The Lost Letters of Heloise and Abelard" *4*
    The Future *5*
    Alone in the Woods for the Rest of the Winter *6*
    The In-Breath *7*
    Unsung *8*
    Chasing the Good Life *9*
    Disclosure *10*
    Seeing Is Believing *11*
    Departure *12*
    Leaving for the Arctic, Listening to My Lover Sing the Blues *14*

IF ONLY A HOUSE STOOD JUST FOR ITSELF
    House-Hunting: 92 Freshwater Road *17*
    House-Hunting: 202 Topsail Road *18*
    House-Hunting: 81 Sycamore Street *19*
    Wanderlust *20*
    Making an Offer *21*
    Anxiety Dreams *22*
    Telepathy: Living Across from the Church *23*
    Robin *25*
    Ascent *27*
    Writing Poetry *29*
    The Here and Now *30*
    Acquainted with the Night *31*
    Dog-Eared *32*

TALKING OR NOT TALKING
    Scrabble 37
    The Other Side of the Coin 38
    Thank You for Not Smoking 39
    Touch and Go 40
    The Metamorphoses' Metamorphosis 41
    Language Travelogue 42
    Winter Landscape: Reading Gertrude Stein 44
    Silhouette 45
    Deontology 46
    Raphael Hythloday Arrives from Utopia 47
    Talking 48
    Not Talking 49

THE DREAM WORLD
    Natural Selection 53
    The Maps of the Labrador Arrive 54
    Poor Me 55
    Ethics 56
    Aesthetics 57
    Gone Fishing 58
    The Out-Breath 59
    Childhood 60
    The Cosmos: Reading Lacan 61
    Prints 62
    The Crossing 63
    Study for Mortality: Charcoal on Paper 64
    Premonition 65
    The Dream World 66

        Acknowledgements 69
        Notes 71

ALONE IN THE WOODS FOR THE REST OF THE WINTER

THE HINTERLAND

I walk as far as I can,
then farther, past
the chain-link barring the road,
tire tracks deep as the rut in my thinking,
the place I always get stuck.
Wanting more, or wanting
less, to be rid of the word
called wanting. Boulders,
tall grass, shrubs I can't name,
birds I can't name, the ocean.
Being a stranger sneaks me through the latch
of language – briefly. Bottles, I know.
Condoms, I know. And the weight
of being human where other humans have been.
Back of the sea like one line of thought,
slight variation of foam at the shore
where artifice gives itself up. Farther out,
a ledge in the rock
as though attention might help. Turning
for home, hands in my pockets, night mists
like animal breath, the black-brown shapes
of gathering mammals
bending to drink at the silent pool
of mind submerged in mind.
If a gap exists at all, it's there
I might have slipped through.

FULL MOON: *Reading "The Lost Letters of Heloise and Abelard"*

A portal. A circular door to forever,
rebirth – a hole to crawl through
leaving failure behind. Call the place we land in
heaven, although it's dark: *the moon does not shine
without the sun.* The two-faced sky
sees both sides, its single eye
trained on absence: words not said,
the back of a mirror, the stars' mirror-image
held on the sea. We paddle through
our own reflections, moon above, a watery
gate. The shape of you, the shape
of me. That infinite distance to cross.

THE FUTURE

I dress for fate: my plastic
pearls, my heels bejewelled
for dancing. You wear a cloak
of stars and moons and gloves
sewn out of satin. The party's
dark, which hinders my chances,
my hope that our orbits collide.
A smoky wind blows in off the terrace,
blocks the view of what-comes-next,
the way the dealer's poker face
obscures the future's features.
He looks at us blandly and shuffles
the years. Everyone's drunk.
Everyone's gambling. We choose
another game and form a ring that stands
for time. We sit on the floor, cross-legged.
I catch your eye across from mine.
Set the bottle spinning.

ALONE IN THE WOODS FOR THE REST OF THE WINTER

I wake and the fire in the woodstove's gone out.
The valley filling with snow. Branches lift
slender arms to pull on lambswool sweaters.
I stand in the kitchen in bare feet and long johns,
nudging the ashes low in the grate. Something flares:

the thought of the man at the party who called me
lovely – I couldn't help blushing, turning away.
This morning is long with coffee and reading,
snow sifting silently down – the window spotlights
fat flakes falling, slow and bright

as comets. Maples gleam, spruce trees gleam,
the river's throat is collared with ice. The gravel road
disappears altogether. Staying strangers keeps the spark
of mystery alight. Alone in the woods for the rest
of the winter – my heart glinting bright in the ash.

THE IN-BREATH

Here's the other side of waiting:
what you don't write writes you.

How about silence, late in the season,
holding its tongue in its teeth; drawing

you like ink through a pen. Meanwhile winter
shies up the path, one girl arriving

at the boys' party, present of paradox
tied with a bow concealed

behind her back. *The sky becomes one
with its clouds, the waves with their mist.*

Even when narrative flings itself free
a net of meaning holds.

UNSUNG

Candid light forsakes the cliff. Balsamic moon, tight-lipped.
You want to go to the land to learn as Simone Weil went
to the factory – you want more than gesture, but only kneeling
lowers you down to silence's field, the nave furred over
with inches of snow. Several prayer books down from breath,
the hymn of particular language. You are there with ten thousand
words, your mouth a leaky cup. Every offering flawed, flawed –
still you fear giving them up. You fear the sin of speech minus
listening, listening with only the ears: a wilder *hush*
of wind through grass, land brushing out her long hair. Goldenrod,
cattails down the back path. Later the ocean like unstudied Latin.
You'll need to stay much longer than planned, to hold your tongue
in your palm; to wait in the unsung blue-black of dusk
before writing anything down. Your driftwood heart so quick
to ignite – huddle around its thin flicker. Light-years back,
the house of language, one round window lit – it's time to turn
your back on home. Time to begin the long translation.

CHASING THE GOOD LIFE

The skinny slick of fame dries up and leaves a sweet relief –
head to the valley and sit by the fall of the stream getting over itself.
The other shore's close, but walled off by water. You're after
a glimpse, a brief apparition of nowhere and nothing that humbles
you down. Squint ahead: a shape in the aspen shucks the form
of doe or moose; it scales the ridge of memory's shadow, swiftly
disappearing. Force yourself to stay cross-legged, night spilling ink
through the grass. A chill settles over your arms. Something makes
its presence known like piano-notes moving through a dark church –
a single hand travelling, slow, up the keys. Silence right after,
the deafening kind, the water's mind gone still. A tail
breaks the surface. Thought ripples out. Sit until blackness
fills all the blanks – the far shore ripped out like a stitch.

DISCLOSURE

If it were only a matter
of looking. If the gaze
could raise its object

high in the air like a player
preparing to slap the puck
into the back of, right

in the nick of, into the net of
time. Things end. Things
peel back to show themselves

as clothing falls to show
the skin, the body's one-way
glass concealing what

it won't allow –
the gut's vague hunch;
the spleen, both kinds,

especially sadness. Open,
I face you, watch your eyes
take in my heart's two eyes,

one blind. The double edge
of lust divides. You see.
You see right through me.

SEEING IS BELIEVING

The handsome doctor fills my frames
with different lenses: better or worse?

An answer's required, though I've learned
beauty is built in back of the brain.

I know this in the hazy way
I know about blood vessels, orbiting

planets. My vision's a blur
of cosmic detritus. I press my face to his metal machine

and tell him, forcefully, *better*. Outside,
I blink against science's shine. The sun lights up

my new-found sight; the optic nerve
plugs into my mind. God is in

the beholder's eye – who else could push
that red ball of fire through the sky?

DEPARTURE

At midnight, the sun is a showgirl in sequins,
too drunk to drag from the stage. Her place makes light

of permanence – an outpost town, a point
of departure – everything poised and ready to leave,

a disappearing act. But first the sun returns again
for some uncalled-for curtain call, lifts anew to show

her lustre, never having set. These float planes too,
paused in the bay, a clutch of cockpits and silver

crescendo, seem helium-prone, at the end of their strings,
ready and raring to rise. But something's wrong: a crowd

draws close, all push and shove around the wharf. A metal bird
lost its nerve a hundred feet above the water – hesitated –

and, of course, in hesitating, fell. The pilot tells
of some rogue wind that grabbed the plane and tore

its wing, then threw it down, a small child's toy,
into the choppy lake. All survived: miracle?

Testimony to the pilot's skill? Early tomorrow this same man
is set to fly us out. Out of where – our selves? Our skins? –

Perhaps he'll take us deeper into something raw
and menacing. The fallen craft, hoisted dry, displayed

on this unstable dock, one arm missing, sunk and gone,
reminds us of our gamble. Were the plane a wishbone, cracked,

we'd hold our short, unlucky half and wonder what it tells about
our impending fate; about redemption's starting point –

is brokenness the only place from where we might be lifted?
We picture ascending up through the ether, a ravel of white

unrolling behind us, ribbon of smoke, visible mark of everywhere
we've been. Is this the wish of every bride who trails a train

down the aisle? And what about the what-comes-next;
the plane's stalled hover, horrible tumble, giant cosmic

fun-fair ride, passengers screaming wide-eyed? Tomorrow
we will rise, like them, trusting the pilot's doubtful credentials,

and though it's late, we feel awake, alert to what's ahead:
another day when we must risk our temporary natures. Another

way, the flight's our calling, forecast of our final trip
high into our human failure. Our terrible, dazzling falling.

LEAVING FOR THE ARCTIC, LISTENING TO MY LOVER SING THE BLUES

If it should ever happen that
I lose my way and winter arrives,
my heart contracting,
thin and white, turning
for another; or if the barrens take me up
like history takes an unknown year
making of me a circle of rocks
with nothing in the centre;
or if the light that fractures blue
into a million rivers and ponds,
in a final act of surrender,
gets in my eyes and blinds me,
wait for me at the piano.
I will know the tips of your fingers
softly on my inner thigh,
your back that bends, releases, bends
over what's open before it.
I will know you by your sounds –
rough and sweet at the back of your throat –
I will know your hard luck song
and it will sing me home.

IF ONLY A HOUSE STOOD JUST FOR ITSELF

HOUSE-HUNTING: *92 Freshwater Road*

You cannot keep your eyes off
the owner, ring through her nose, braid
down her back like a length of rope

you could climb. *Save me. Let down
your hair.* Your words are chewed up
in the garbage disposal she's using

to woo you. You need a friend.
She calls you honey –
it tempts you to sign. Kitchen

features a built-in dishwasher,
stove she is willing to leave.
She needs to move now –

she wants to be *gone*.
You, of course, take this personally.
Back at home the flashing red light

is just a wrong number, a hang-up.
You're porous, lachrymose, social-life
starved – but hip

to the law of supply and demand.
You want to buy. She wants to sell.
Both of you human, no less.

HOUSE-HUNTING: *202 Topsail Road*

Great house for kids, the owner says gaily,
and stares at the flat of your stomach as though
it will now begin rising like bread. A punch

in the gut of intention and you're doubled over.
From the top floor, sunset's view,
your old life sinking too. Use the closet

off the master to shelter the egg
of your dream for yourself; a crack
in the shell of your armour and longing

weeps through. Whatever you ache for,
this isn't it. But your breasts start to leak
and your hands begin searching – fuse box, cellar,

under the sink – opening every dark hole
of the future. Hide-and-seek, or maybe sardines,
this is like finding four or five bodies

crammed in the crawl space under the floor,
the instant of fear before recognition:
is that what you're looking for? Is it?

HOUSE-HUNTING: *81 Sycamore Street*

When you mention this street, no one knows its name.
On the map it is lined in with careful grey pencil:
it smudges beneath your wet thumb. Weeds
in the yard. Chicken-wire fence. Step over

razors, needles, syringes, your lover's hand hot
in the small of your back,
a parent persuading a child.
Windows stare wanly, pupils dilated –

the front door sighs open, ready to welcome,
slams in a sharp gust of wind.
Inside, your eyes blink hard to adjust
to a cliché of dust, sheets over chairs. Light bulbs

blown out. Each door reveals another dark room,
nesting dolls shrinking in size. *This could be a study,*
says the Real Estate Man. Trying to convince you, and himself.
You send the Real Estate Man to the car, and kiss your lover –

his tongue is on fire. Steady wail of sirens closing in.
House of your nightmares. House of your dreams.
You cannot say which is stronger: desire
to fix it up, or desire for decay.

WANDERLUST

Next things to learn are the routes out of town.
Clearly, the humpback off Freshwater Bay is just
a red herring, the width of its tail obscuring your view
like a blindfold. So many sights you aren't meant

to see: squint, and the sea disappears. Nude and alone
in the tide pool at Flatrock – a man walks by, hands
in his pockets, swivels the compass of his face
away from the blight of your breasts. Nothing here's

female. Sky: an Old Testament God. Eternal
fog has the warden's approval,
unlike you with your self-absorbed lines,
wandering far off the marked path of logic. Only

the Real Estate Man with his locks and his leather
might drag you back. Something's building,
some kind of craving, thirst that starts in the treads
of your sneakers, sets you searching long miles

of coastline, trail thinning out like a vein.
First time in years you've got something to lose.
The way to survive: unscrew your heart
and swallow the contents each hour.

MAKING AN OFFER

Dead Man's Pond, above St. John's:
how the lights from the city drop,
pieces of clothing we flick off and shiver
away from, exposed. How the water pricks
our skin, reminds us of its name. If only

a house stood just for itself; had only one window,
one clapboard wall, a single door opening
in. If it were simple as signing a form,
awaiting a stranger's reply. If only our hope
was not that loon, calling out once,

disappearing. We are divers, deep-down explorers.
We're back-of-the-mind diviners.
Missing home while running from home,
we are black towels, wrung out but wet, heavy
with waiting, with weight. How it feels to name

desire, how little we have to give back.
We're a first mortgage, a second. If only
after achieving the goal, there wasn't this dip
of regret. House, loon, lights blinking
out: look: they were here. Now they're gone.

ANXIETY DREAMS

The day plumps up with what's undone,
rises like dough. We punch it down.
We save our kisses in a safe that's fat and pink
but void of coins, and so we make
a run for bed, pull the blankets
over our heads. It makes the darkness
no more dark. The pet we don't own
nuzzles her face into our choice:
stay put, or don't. Nothing moves,
until a shadow lifts a finger, as if in thought.
I think, for a minute, our problems are solved.
Problems, you ask. What problems?

TELEPATHY: *Living Across from the Church*

The steeple bell breaks open
the hour – two parts, four,
a head-aching twenty,
a mind-splitting forty, a migraine
beginning just when you lose count –

a pause. The street flicks back into focus,
parked cars stunned and holding
their tongues. Eternity flutters,
caught in the gutter like some discarded
church bulletin, and you too, darling,

pause at your desk, a deadline looming,
staring you down.
You've not slept for days.
You raise your pencil over your notebook,
maestro before a momentous

beginning, conductor's baton
aloft in the air, a signal some angel
spots: on cue
the bell recommences its bold brassy band,
breaking the hour more fervently now

like bread for the masses
who stream from the church to slam
their car doors and shout at their children –
there's no need to speak, my love.
I hear what you're thinking.

ROBIN

She must have thought this cabin empty
(which, for weeks at a time, it is) to set her cup

of twig and twine, like a glass of pricey wine,
a golden goblet, gently down in the eave above

the door. It seemed enough. She plucked its warmth
from Easter's closet, fashioned it from fleece and leaf

and in it laid her regal prize, out of reach of porcupines
and other probing eyes. Our wheels up gravel:

sad surprise. She refuses, first, to yield and stays, puffed up,
all huff and flush, ensconced next to the "Welcome" sign –

a sulky host – but as the car is unpacked, slow, (as though
a complex line of thought), and as the door keeps slamming closed

an inch away from her abode, some base instinct
makes her leave her nest for good and save herself;

makes her swoop, a blazing breast, over to the maple's safety.
Beady gaze stays glued on us. Human will, says Augustine,

is poised between a kind of hell and good that looks
like feathered flight: the heart's sharp urge to rise and hover

over nature's endless picture. Yes, to love it all. Now
(the trunk relieved of beer and snacks and sleeping bags)

we let the digital camera help: tippy-toed, we reach its eye
above her hearth too high for sight, then bring the slim box

down and crowd around its wordless snap. Selfishly,
we hope to see the absence left by winter's death;

that hollow nest, deep and tough, and from it, thrusting up,
the root of spring returned as form. Three blue eggs.

Three perfect globes. And in the morning, once we've risen,
three round dreams, eyes closed tight and beaks agape,

dashed in shells across the deck. We stand, astonished,
coffee cooling, all around us sun and breeze unspooling green

between the maple's flip, indifferent leaves. Robin's gone.
Her brood's been eaten. Though it's resurrection's season,

I don't wish for them to rise, but, for once, for words that find
some meaning I can get behind: oh yolky blot. Oh yellow

slick. Let me stand and take their place, be this mess
I've helped make; be broken, spilled, forgiven.

ASCENT

Forgive me?

No.

An angled reminder,
your two-letter answer, a rock in my boot,

a cramp. The hike now steeper
and clearer in scope.

Please?

Silence. A sky full of gulls –
there's some dying thing on the beach

they're in love with. They circle,
circle. All at once,

plummet – ripping the ropey red life
from its wound. We're pulled apart

at the heart of our natures,
hinge between water

and sky. Gulls stitch the gap,
dragging our insides

up through the gape between bowls of blue,
ocean and air, that infinite

absence. The high shrill squabble
of hunger. *Forgive me*, I ask you.

The winged gods are feeding.

Heaven? An echo:

Forgive me.

WRITING POETRY

She sewed him a boat out of birchbark
and thread. A gift in the flow
of her steady affection, one moment freighted
with many. Perfect

and useless, it sat on their shelf,
unfit to weather the rising of water.
Too small to stand up to anything
real. Now it seems

a magical vessel, able to travel
upstream, back in time. A tiny
reminder: the heart slips its anchor.
She's glad she has something to keep.

THE HERE AND NOW

Stuck on an island of unmoving hours,
forever is ours for the keeping. The present:

a glut of perpetual pleasure, gladness we gather
from each grain of sand, from beach-glass and seashell

and every pale wing: the hawk floating out to encircle
the dusk; even the horsefly that lands on my forehead,

fulfilling its fate – that sting. Red rises up
from campfire light and hovers, the twin

of a sun that can't set. Stranded in time,
the tide slips away like an unwanted guest

at a wedding. We marry the moment and promise
our faith. You heap me with sand, right up to my neck.

The game binds me tight to the *here* and the *now*,
the itch on my forehead, sun's fiery

match. Too late, I realize the sting of nostalgia,
my hands buried, cannot be scratched.

ACQUAINTED WITH THE NIGHT

Longing hurts and pleases.
Two more months of snow. Streets
crawl under blankets again; eyes closed tight,
empty storefronts are children waiting
to be tucked in. Nobody comes. Storm after storm
releases loss into slightly deeper banks, and quiet
flakes through streetlamp light brings to mind
the bedtime story of my oldest love returned,
at last, from all those years. Once, drunk,
dating someone else, you held my hand in a cab.
I want to go back to that kind of wanting
and you not wanting me back.

DOG-EARED

I fold down the tips of my memory's book.
The page where we sat on the porch before dawn,
listing the guests for our wedding – marriage
remote as a tropical country, one we would never
discover. I mark the humid Guyanese dusk,
my hammock strung between two trees, a heat wave
hung, thick and building, there between
our bodies. I came to your window,
your mother asleep, and mark your bed,
bed of your boyhood – not the kissing, but pressing our faces
together, the shield we would make. Remember?
Holding our hands up to keep the world out.
The radio rustled, low in that dark. Waterloo nights.
Nothing could stop us. No wall of pleasure
would get in our way. Pushing and tunnelling
into each other, trying to puncture the bliss.
We knew we would need to break it to keep it,
to barrel through into the *real*, the adult –
to ruin our artlessness, squander our luck.
The last place is dog-eared before we knew pain.
Then, the pages of unruly scrawl,
sentences struck, the pen tearing through,
tear-stains, pleading, my unmeant cruelty,
your unmeant cruelty. Then blankness.
Waiting for years for what we had earned
while time's bold parade passed us by.
The final installment – *I wish I could tell you* –

the rest of our future, unwritten. A crumble
of petals between the last pages.
The red rose you gave me.
The remnants.

TALKING OR NOT TALKING

SCRABBLE

I'll tell you a secret: I'm making this up
out of the letters I drew. Everything written
is just *provision*, the word now sprawled
across the corner of the board:
a triple-word score. Still,
the wine cannot conceal the little failures
we both know: the X in *hex* – just been played –
falls short of expectation. Let me say I love
the way you lay your tiles with such abandon,
slapping them into their slots
like signs accepting
meaning. Because, tonight, the game implies
that things *may* be the way they seem,
that spelling out the lack in language
won't result in less. *Less*, well-placed, makes *liver
sliver*, conjures up that slip-of-a-moon, the one
that dangles from the sky
as image hangs from speech.
The way your glance makes *more* of me;
slide your R in next to my E. We'll build
a ladder of consummate
pleasure, one long vowel at a time.

THE OTHER SIDE OF THE COIN

The nuns live on the edge of town
overlooking a lake. They take
turns cooking, dress in slacks.

I stay for a week, descend into silence
which soon overflows with what it refutes.
In bed, my breath writes notes to the night,

small puffs of steady contentment. Drifting off,
I bask in the inkling of pleasures piled up
like layers of cake; I open wide into a dream

about the sullen retreater beside me
whose sulky demeanour takes shape in the wall
between his room and my own. The same lake

lies east of our windows – nevertheless, our views
diverge. Morning arrives, a stamp on its corner,
an airmail letter slid under my door.

Rain shimmies down its thin silver pole.
I stroll the ambit of my mind, gathering gladness
like seashells and whelk, and find

the man inured to angst evokes in me
a giddy thanks. The wall between us
joins us – I count on him for my existence.

THANK YOU FOR NOT SMOKING

On the seventh day Solitude comes to my door
with a bottle of cheap scotch
and matches. It lights an inferno

and banishes me in the fashion
of Plato with poets. So much for use.
So long, you beauty. Outside,

I trample a path to the pasture. Cattle,
untended, their udders distended,
moo at the honey-and-milk

of the moon, that monocle leaking
lacteal light. Suddenly blinded,
I wander afield, fingers outstretched

like ten small antennae
and find myself back at the site of the fire,
one I can sense but not see. Solitude

smells like an unseemly lover,
cigarette smouldering deep in the blankets,
a lover I wish that I'd never

invited. But how to assert this considerately?
I practise, repeating, *I need to be alone.*
Solitude, it isn't you, it's me.

TOUCH AND GO

Friday shucks off
work-week shackles,
busts out of its prison.
Booze on your breath,
you press me up

against the bar
and force me to choose:
life, or art.
I'm whisked by taxi
back to my room

and fall on the bed,
head reeling. I swallow
the moon like an aspirin.
Lit from within with liquor's
speed I need you

in my bloodstream.
Addict's bargain:
I'll choose life
but only if you
choose me.

THE METAMORPHOSES' METAMORPHOSIS

It would be easy to call me the violet,
to say my face shadows you
morning to night
as Clytie's was said to shadow
the sun. Let's take Ovid for his word,
follow his myth across the horizon
the way a jealous, lustlorn girl might
dog her heartthrob's every move,
refuse to take her eyes off him,
to shift out of his steady heat, and so
sprout roots, a flower's face. Petals
plucked out one by one, the story wobbles
on its stem, meaning changed
in every telling: loves me, loves me
not.

LANGUAGE TRAVELOGUE

Words bleached white,
hollowed out. Cups,

the steaming stream
of time, how we hide in the heart's

excuse. The truth: we know
the secret code but keep it

to ourselves. We cross our legs,
take small sips, smiling, our lips

pressed together. Nervous passengers
boarding a train, pigeons

above in the station's arches,
a brilliant flapping

in back of our eyes. We squint,
say nothing, clutch our passports

against the emptiness
under our ribs. Someone steals

a last goodbye, the briefest kiss,
there – the heavy doors

are bolted closed – there's no guarantee
we'll survive. Farewell to tea

late in October, a loved-one's
parting words. Farewell, farewell to

everything looted: the empty
jewel-box. The mouth.

WINTER LANDSCAPE: *Reading Gertrude Stein*

> *As I say a noun is a name of a thing, and therefore slowly if you feel what is inside that thing you do not call it by the name by which it is known.*

Topsail beach, early December, all of the tourists long gone –
move out past the man-made stairs, the lookout's bruised black eye.
You are a stranger whose bumbling comes from the fat lip of trying
to name: the ocean isn't a mirror held up to the damage of sun
in the pines. A hiss in the underbrush up on the cliff and the trail
lopes sideways, down to the rocks – you'll need to hike in several
kilometres past your craving to get it all down. First thin crust
of winter's glass, the same encasement as language: a shine
so bright you can barely see through it. The quiet popping
of ice in spruce. You can't hear the trees' real names.

SILHOUETTE

The words of the elms have fallen.

Loss speaks in frost, that careful lace,
white-gloved fingers
reaching. All the selves you couldn't hold

come back to your window now,
frozen children wanting in,
voices loose in the dusk.

Snipped from the clouds, the day drifts down –

grief is the shadow it casts.

You turn away from the one who calls.
Her mittens pressed to the glass.

DEONTOLOGY

The fledgling ethicists, forced
to school, fold their hands at their desks.

Ten minds perk like coffee pots,
turned on and promptly forgotten.

Teacher is busy bestowing gold stars
for compliance, submission;

behind her back, little Nietzsche
aims to copy Hegel's paper.

Teacher shoots a look that says:
duty requires you do what's right!

God is Dead, Friedrich replies, and bonks
young Georg over the head with a robot.

RAPHAEL HYTHLODAY ARRIVES FROM UTOPIA

He tells the story of his town
where things aren't owned
but rather bound and

passed around: a manuscript,
a book among infinite readers.
A crimeless land, no poverty,

shared property, no upper class.
We wonder: can this place *exist*?
He's homesick but he aims to convince,

groups us here in one big ring
to talk through all our doubts.
Someone brings up opposites –

we turn to beg his answer:
where is the *pleasure* in life without sorrow?
Hythloday?

Sir?

Are you there?

TALKING

Someone thinks a steady voice implies a steady self.
How, he asks, could humans exist in absence of some solid core?
He sees this like an apple's spine, the sweet flesh bitten away.

His neighbour says the self is spread like seeds throughout
the centre; like separate personalities, or fruit throughout a tree.

A woman in bangles tosses the trope – the core thuds into the trash.
She wipes her hands on the back of her jeans and names the pull
of Reason; points out just how language serves, translating

concept to sign. This is swiftly refuted (of course):
there's no removed viewpoint to stand on. The woman persists:
she *knows* she exists. She pinches her cheeks. *Here I am!*

A voice in the corner: *What about trauma? Doesn't it shatter
the self?* Talk turns fast to tight-lipped texts,

always holding back. It's all downhill from here. The setting sun
applies itself to table, chalkboard, percolator, painting the room
a unified pink. For a moment, the fragments look whole.

NOT TALKING

When you leave I go to the wood
that wears its being like a loose down
vest. Windfall, deadfall, I duck under
words, the quiet forest assembling itself
around the thought of thought. Lie in the snow,
my face turned up. Somewhere close,
the river's mouth is choked with last fall's
leaves. Nothing left to say about
all our endless nothing-said, talking
held in place of touch like slides held up
to light. Naked maples, empty-handed,
reach toward that potent height where
things unseen return as form. Magic
trick, mysterious flicker: you turn and take
my hand. Lead me down the trampled trail
where language beat a fast retreat;
show me the hollow behind your heart
where all the cold's pressed down.
We're up to our knees now, headed for silence.
Come and lie down with me there.

THE DREAM WORLD

NATURAL SELECTION

The black sleeve of history is rolled at the cuff.
Beneath it, a flash of red silk. Say it's the red
of someone's umbrella – a woman at the bus stop,
already late. Say the rain is pocking the gutter,
the gutter is rushing, unstoppable: fate?
Empedocles saw the start of the world
as chaos with body parts floating around it.
Think of pure blackness; a foot sailing past.
At the far end of town a man turns the key,
backs down his driveway, craning behind him.
The woman gives up and decides she will walk.
The rain is still falling like what's coming next:
at some point the foot will collide with a leg.
The man hits the brakes and the car hydroplanes
into a version of what we expect, smack of the male
up against female. Love was the glue, Empedocles said –
but let's call it chance. Let's say the year is 1831:
a man boards a ship, bound for a future he's never
imagined. Restless and bored, unmoored and drifting,
his uncle has pushed him to take the position.
He's pleased with his title, repeats it to himself.
Charles Darwin: captain's companion.

THE MAPS OF THE LABRADOR ARRIVE

The first expedition: 1903.
Leonidas Hubbard, George Ellison, Dillon Wallace
set out for the Naskapi hunting grounds,
hoping to find the caribou herd,
enough meat for the winter.

Thousands of miles of uncharted forest,
blackflies swarming their noses and mouths,
trap-like tangle of willow and alder
reaching and pulling them down.

Must not all things be swallowed up in death?

My paddle, my single canoe.

POOR ME

Three days camped at the edge of this lake,
summer light of a dime-store novel, that gauzy softness
dusk can make. Lonesome, heartsick. Now,

after dinner, after the loon has opened her songbook,
started in practising scales, after I've poured
a shot of whiskey under one raised eyebrow of moon
nursing my ache for the people I miss and after darkness

unfolds its wings, prepares its descent: a moose.
Hooves the size of salad plates, legs
the height of my shoulders. He walks, regally,

out of the woods, as though arriving fashionably late,
then swims the narrow channel leisurely,
antlers high and proud. He climbs the bank,
hindquarters bulging, an athlete going up for a medal.

One minute later he's gone. The moose is nothing less
and nothing more than temporary –
and yet there's mud marking the surface where

halfway across he paused. What to make
of his slow glance behind him, the single blink of eyes?
He took in the lake's unflinching reflection,
the rippled blaze, clear and pink, of the season's

imminent end. Then he turned his gaze
on me. A simple gesture to summer light.
Look, it asked. Do you see?

ETHICS

The field guide shows a stork-like bird
whose likeness I fold
from Japanese paper.

The careful work demands a mind
with as many complex pleats,
the kind of mind we elevate

to the height of flight.
Meanwhile snow geese
migrate for miles to reach

their nesting grounds. They angle
through the dull white sky, wedging
winter open. High ground gone,

simple instinct slides them south
at season's end, a gosling
with a broken breastbone left behind

to die. My own heart flutters
at this ousting, wings
held out like an origami crane's.

Why the ache to fly with the flock?
Smooth out the paper:
my animal creases remain.

AESTHETICS

A rotting cod, the shine
of spine, the skeletal secret
named in sleep, and in

that other, sounder sleep
that gleams like wet sand,
unto itself, as though

in wanting nothing at all
the glint of something
appeared. The water

tosses, turns in its bed,
tide's wide blanket
thrown briefly back:

form without use, backbone
of beauty, washed up
on shore, picked clean.

GONE FISHING

The rainbow trout has lost its life
and stays, mounted, liquids drained,
displayed atop the fireplace, a foot above
that steady flame like some protracted
hell. Heaven, for this fluid one, existed

as a quiet pool, a place where something swift,
piscine, could slide beneath the water's
ceiling, elude the rod ingeniously
as in the truth of dreams.
For three months the river narrowed,

tied its thread round summer's finger,
reminder of oxygen's final failure –
how we'll all hang, one eye glassed,
some reluctant trophy. Take the fish above
the mantle – vigour dimmed, snuffed-out

wick – why should I be different?
Yet faced with death I somehow see
my own escape, a sweet release,
a swish receding through the reeds –
the one that slips away.

THE OUT-BREATH

The cabin at dusk is the body, contained.
Tall grass slopes down into sleep. From here
the stream that slips through the willow: a visible
ribbon of longing, of time. To cast without
intent to catch; to stand on the bank of a beautiful
ending, fireflies floating out over the water,
lost children swinging their lanterns.

CHILDHOOD

Triscuits, cheese cubes, fingers
of celery, cool grooves filled
with peanut butter – sourdough,

made by my mother's hand,
the starter yeasty, stored
in the dark. The plate appeared

at noon precisely,
cleaving the day into unequal halves,
an apple split, then split again, a wedge per year

of life so far. School was approaching,
reckoning day. I drank my milk
and knew the world

as child-sized bites to cram in my mouth,
token bits of something bigger. Late
at night the world was lost, the way

a hunger fills and empties, plate
or planet, round and white:
look up. Look up and marvel.

THE COSMOS: *Reading Lacan*

The baby is learning
to eat soft foods. Fruit
of experience puréed
by father, simplified into
minuscule mouthfuls that manage,
still, like wayward missiles,
to miss their target and splatter
the faces of innocent
children. This one here
begins to glean that evening
means betrayal. Meal adjourned,
bathed and changed, kissed
and laid in the cell of his crib,
his hunger remains. He fits his fist
into its shape, fills his face
with fingers. That other flesh,
that milky moon, comes less often,
sets too early – mobile above
a stellar distraction, wild constellation
cleaving the cosmos, baby peers up
from the crux of his cradle,
mouth as wide as its absence.
He searches the spheres like
an early astronomer starting
to question his central position;
unsure what exactly he's lost
but already desperate to find it.

PRINTS

Late afternoon, alone in the trees,
the quiet creak of skis through snow,
a shy approach, your stealth.
A pattered line of rabbit prints

veers off into evening.
Think of shadow, someone
leaving, somebody else bedding down.
This kind of softness brushes your shoulders,

keeps your secrets
safe. *Hush, hush*, your human tracks;
your binding's metal tick; you're moving through

the natural world and understanding
nothing. Day's last sun gives up the fight
like something in you

sacrificed, something bright that glints like blood
staining the snow beneath the trap,
that melts in ice and light on spruce and finally
ends as glistening.

THE CROSSING

The snowshoe dreams a frozen lake
as the mind dreams thought –
pulled inside out, a mitten drying
next to a campfire. You've crossed the ice,

a dim line of reason: turning, turning
and doubling back. Finding your way,
losing it. Birch bear witness,
arms thrown up. The snowshoe dreams

a quiet mind where breaking trail
leaves no mark, a sharpened cold as dusk
drifts in, woodsmoke over the lake.
You draw your knees up to your chest,

hold yourself as night holds day.
The final light leaks out. It leaves
its pink and gentleness on the snow
you've come across: the broken surface
thinking leaves. The endless criss-crossed tracks.

STUDY FOR MORTALITY: *Charcoal on Paper*

Woodsmoke drifts across the cove
like memory rising off the mind.

What's left is thought, and deeper, *being*,
that shimmering coal in a heap of ash.

You turn for home across the low hills –

three or four houses scattered behind you,
a child's toys hastily abandoned
in favour of the eternal life.

PREMONITION

The early snow-removal trucks
arrive like liberating troops. Up and up
the streets they charge to roses tossed
from windows. Winter's a war almost won.
Throw back the drapes: warmth sashays in,
a kink, little inkling: we've felt this before,
forgotten it too, in the womb, in an earlier

life. Dreaming is easy in hours like these,
the mind's backyard awash in new light,
but troops are troops, welcomed or not.
Still I haven't said what I mean: something lost
will clear a space for something new to follow.
Ice in the harbour, for instance, melting,
starts the swell of spring. The Quakers,

for instance, worship in silence that breaks
in an outburst of words. The shattered things,
which is to say the cool of your palm against
my thigh, which is to say there is no saying
for the dark and shady. No perfection.
My broken parts have always been broken –
touch me. Touch me there.

THE DREAM WORLD

Shake up envy. Shake up
the impulse toward acquisition –
it batters you nightly, a moth at a bulb.
Shake up the trope of the moth at a bulb:

words take shape in fresh combination,
cheerleaders on court at half-time. A girl
tossed skyward, bent at the waist, a check mark
against a ballot's blank box. Vote for the moment,

vote for atonement, for taking a long walk alone
through the forest. Morning is raising
its snapping white flag. You exit the alders, hands
in the air, and wake: your final surrender.

ACKNOWLEDGEMENTS

These poems, often in different versions, first appeared in *Arc, The Malahat Review, Grain, The New Quarterly, CV2, The Columbia Poetry Review, PRISM International, Atlas, Descant, Prairie Fire*, and in the anthology *Breathing Fire II: Canada's New Poets*. Several were published in the online journals *nth position* and *slingshot*, and others in *The Current, The Walrus*, and the *Globe and Mail*. "Winter Landscape," under the title "December," and accompanied by an image by the brilliant Will Gill, was published as a "poemphlet" by Running the Goat Press in St. John's in 2005.

The House-Hunting poems were commissioned for the 2004 CBC Poetry Face-Off, recorded on a CD of the same title, and broadcast on *Sounds Like Canada*. Ten others, under the title "The Mind's Eye," won first prize in the 2005 CBC Literary Awards, were broadcast on *Between the Covers* and published in *enRoute Magazine*. "Robin" was an Editor's Choice in the 2006 Arc Poem of the Year Contest, and a finalist in the 2007 National Magazine Awards.

Thanks to the Canada Council for the Arts for financial assistance, to the City of St. John's, and to the Newfoundland and Labrador Arts Council for its generosity throughout the duration of our stay in Newfoundland. Thanks to the Humanities Department at Memorial University, especially to Peter Trnka and Peter Harris, to the Banff Centre for the Arts, and to John Barton for the timely encouragement in his capacity as the former editor of *Arc*. To Steven Heighton, Suzanne Buffam, Michael Crummey, Mark Callanan, Sarah Wiseman, David Seymour, Alayna Munce, and Susan Ingersoll, who commented on earlier versions of the poems. To Ellen Seligman, Anita Chong, and Ruta Liormonas at McClelland &

Stewart. To my family, and to Degan Davis in particular, who has shaped this book and its author on every level.

I am extremely grateful to Molly Peacock for her astute edit, to Lynn Henry for her continued support, and to Don McKay and Anne Simpson for their feedback on the manuscript as a whole. Finally I would like to acknowledge Chris Hutchinson whose patience and insight were invaluable.

Did I mention Chris Hutchinson? Thanks Chris.

"Leaving for the Arctic, Listening to My Lover Sing the Blues" is for Degan. "Dog-Eared" is for Matt. "Childhood" is for Emily.

This book is for my grandparents, Fred and Norma Martin.

NOTES

The first epigraph is taken from *Grimm's Fairy Tales*, by Jacob Grimm and Wilhelm Grimm, translated by Margaret Hunt, Dover Publications, 2007.

The second epigraph is taken from *Collected Works of C.G. Jung, Volume 10: Civilization in Transition*, Princeton University Press, 2nd edition, 1970.

"Acquainted with the Night" borrows its title from Robert Frost.

The italicized line in "The In-Breath" is from Li Qingzhao, as quoted in *Women in Praise of the Sacred: 43 Centuries of Spiritual Poetry by Women*, ed. Jane Hirshfield, HarperCollins, 1994.

The italicized line in "Full Moon" is from *The Lost Love Letters of Heloise and Abelard*, ed. C.J. Mews, St. Martin's Press, 1999.

The italicized line in "The Maps of the Labrador Arrive" is an abbreviated quote from Plato's Phaedo dialogue, *Plato Five Dialogues: Euthyphro, Apology, Crito, Meno, Phaedo*, translated by G.M.A. Grube, Hackett Publishing Company; New Ed edition, 1981.

The epigraph to "Winter Landscape" is from Gertrude Stein's lecture "Poetry and Grammar" in *Look at Me Now and Here I Am: Writings and Lectures 1909–1945*, Penguin Books, 1967.